COUNTRY LIVING

garden
decorating

garden

decorating

ACCENTS
FOR OUTDOORS

by DEBRA MULLER PRICE

foreword by NANCY MERNIT SORIANO

HEARST BOOKS   NEW YORK

Library of Congress Cataloging-in-Publication Data

Price, Debra Muller.
    Garden decorating / Debra Muller Price and the editors of Country Living.
        p. cm.
    ISBN 1-58816-024-6
    1. Garden ornaments and furniture. I. Country living (Firm) II. Title.

SB473.5 .P75 2001
717--dc21

00-053895

Printed in Hong Kong
First Edition
10 9 8 7 6 5 4 3 2 1

Text set in Minion

Photography on pages 6–7, 14–15, 17, 20, 26–27, 28, 29, 30–31, 34–35, 42–43, 48–49,
58–59, 60, 65, 78–79, 81, 82, 82–83, 84–85, 88, 90–91, 92, 93, 94, 95, 102, 112, endpapers,
front cover, back cover (left), spine by Keith Scott Morton; 21, 39, 44–45, 46, 47, 50,
52–53, 54, 55, 56–57, 64, 70, 76, 89, 100–101, 104–105, 106–107, back cover (right)
by Erika R. Shank; 40–41, 61, 68–69, 71, 72, 73, 87 by Jeremy Samuelson; 4–5, 9, 66–67,
77, 80, 103 by Dency Kane; 10, 12–13, 18–19, 37, 38, 74 by William P. Steele; 22, 23,
24–25, 51 by Jessie Walker; 36, 97 by Charles Gold; 108, 109 by Roy Gumpel; 16, 32 by
Mark Lohman; 33 by Debra DeBoise; 62–63 by Barbara Horovitz; 98–99 by Paul Kopelow.

www.countryliving.com

For *Country Living*
Editor-in-Chief, Nancy Mernit Soriano
Art Director, Susan M. Netzel
Deputy Editor, Lawrence A. Bilotti

PRODUCED BY SMALLWOOD AND STEWART, INC., NEW YORK CITY
BOOK DESIGN: AMY HENDERSON

contents

foreword

I'VE WATCHED WITH DELIGHT in recent years as more and more people have embraced gardening as a hobby. It is a passion of mine—one that I inherited from my mother and now hope to pass on to my young son. As the interest in gardening has grown, the boundary between house and garden has begun to blur. A perfect example of this is the rising trend toward using garden collectibles as decorative accents inside the house.

At *Country Living* we believe that the garden can be just as beautifully furnished as any indoor room. In this book we present creative outdoor settings decorated with vintage textiles, cherished heirlooms, and unexpected garden treasures. You'll find that ornament can be anything that adds interest or beauty to the landscape—a weathered birdhouse, an ornate ironwork gate, a colorful wheelbarrow, a fanciful folk-art sculpture, or a simple watering can filled with petunias and phlox. We hope that you'll take inspiration from these pages and cultivate your own personal style in the garden.

—NANCY MERNIT SORIANO, *Editor-in-Chief*

introduction

Hᴏᴡ ʟᴏɴɢ ʜᴀs ɪᴛ ʙᴇᴇɴ sɪɴᴄᴇ ʏᴏᴜ ʜᴏsᴛᴇᴅ an outdoor brunch, sat under a tree to make

an entry in your garden journal, or enjoyed a romantic evening under the stars? If you're like most people, it has

probably been too long. We spend our leisure time mowing the grass and tending to flower beds, but our yards

essentially stand unoccupied for much of the year.

We hope that this book will inspire you to begin living in the garden. It doesn't matter if your property is

large or small, because any lot can be transformed into a year-round pleasure ground for family and friends. On

the following pages we share advice on how to create outdoor rooms and furnish them with beauty and comfort

in mind. Along the way we include tips on planning a garden path, unearthing unique garden accents, dressing

up an ordinary toolshed, and decorating the garden for the winter season. Join us as we explore a number

of memorable gardens and contemplate the endless possibilities that lie just beyond your own back door.

a room
outdoors

"The love of gardening is a seed that once sown never dies," said the legendary English garden designer Gertrude Jekyll. While most of us would agree that gardens bring immense pleasure, we often don't enjoy them to the fullest. We spend countless hours potting, watering,

weeding, and pruning but very little time sitting back and savoring the beauty we've coaxed from nature.

If this sounds familiar, carry your imagination outside and take a fresh look. Think of your yard as an extension of your house, as a series of rooms. When people buy or build a house, they assign each room a function and furnish it accordingly. Often, however, such planning stops at the back door. Decorating in the garden, though, is no different from decorating in the house. Just as indoors, the most successful design projects begin with the bones: the walls, doorways, and other structural details that define a space. Taking the time to get these elements right will surely prevent headaches down the road.

trade your pruners
for a cushion and
relax amid the lush landscape

Blurring the lines: Flowering vines, above, connect a window seat to the garden. Coordinating pillows, opposite, bring indoor comfort to a rustic seating area.

First, make a list of favorite activities. If you like hosting dinner parties, you might want to scatter several small tables beneath a vine-covered pergola. If you crave peace and quiet, carve out a sitting area where you

can make entries in your garden journal; a potting shed can also provide solitude as well as space to pursue your hobby rain or shine. For casual meals and time with children, a fresh-air family room would be ideal.

Next, determine the size of each room and select the necessary structural elements. To make garden rooms feel intimate, you can create living walls with boxwood hedges, perennial borders, and rows of potted plants, or you might construct picket fences and trellises. In a hot or rainy climate, you may require a ceiling. A shade tree often does the trick, but installing a gazebo or setting up market umbrellas when you need them are other good solutions.

Outdoor rooms can be just as comfortable—and as beautifully decorated—as the interior of your home. They can be as formal as a brick terrace or as simple as a few weathered lawn chairs clustered under an old elm tree. The key is to create inviting spaces that beckon you to explore and enjoy your own garden.

PILLOWS IN THE GARDEN

The simple addition of fabric makes outdoor settings more welcoming. Toss a few pillows on a garden bench and suddenly you have a cozy spot for a nap or conversation.

Greenery provides a surprisingly neutral backdrop for color, so don't be afraid to be bold when you're selecting patterns. Botanical prints enliven old wood or twig furniture; stripes look crisp on wicker or poolside metal chairs. To get the look of an old garden, use vintage textiles for pillow covers. New textiles made for outdoor use are a good choice if you're concerned about upkeep. And since even reliable weather forecasters will make mistakes, opt for covers that can easily be removed for laundering or drying.

A greenhouse, opposite, nurtures plants, but it also refreshes a gardener's soul during the winter; prized myrtle topiaries and architectural elements embellish the interior. An old farmhouse porch, above, offers fresh air, cool breezes, and protection from inclement weather. An avid Pennsylvania gardener uses the space as a casual workroom.

even a plain harvest basket or a stack of old clay pots gives beauty and grace to a gardener's shelter

There's nothing quite as serene
as a personal retreat tucked into
the corner of a cottage garden.
A shed, whose primary purpose
is to safeguard supplies, can
also serve as a snug hideaway,
especially when furnished with a
comfortable chair and shelves
of favorite flea-market finds. In
a Colorado garden, left, a simple
plywood toolshed is painted with
charming trompe l'oeil scenes.
The interior, opposite, boasts a
rustic cupboard filled with old
birdhouses, treasured garden
supplies, and a colorful rag rug.

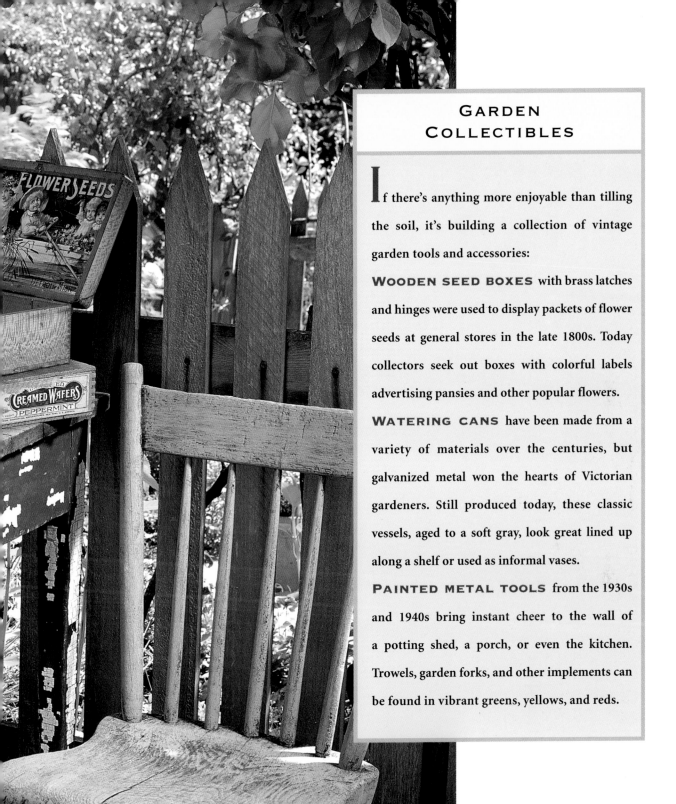

GARDEN COLLECTIBLES

If there's anything more enjoyable than tilling the soil, it's building a collection of vintage garden tools and accessories:

WOODEN SEED BOXES with brass latches and hinges were used to display packets of flower seeds at general stores in the late 1800s. Today collectors seek out boxes with colorful labels advertising pansies and other popular flowers.

WATERING CANS have been made from a variety of materials over the centuries, but galvanized metal won the hearts of Victorian gardeners. Still produced today, these classic vessels, aged to a soft gray, look great lined up along a shelf or used as informal vases.

PAINTED METAL TOOLS from the 1930s and 1940s bring instant cheer to the wall of a potting shed, a porch, or even the kitchen. Trowels, garden forks, and other implements can be found in vibrant greens, yellows, and reds.

furnishing a
living
room
under the sky

keith and Monique Keegan have always enjoyed working in the yard during the summer. But until they installed a brick terrace, the Ohio couple didn't know just how good outdoor living could be. "If you only have a garden, you just walk through and look at it," Keith explains. "But once you have a place to sit down, you tend to congregate in the garden."

Located under the shade of an old pine tree, the terrace serves as a multipurpose space akin to a great room. It's a favorite spot for relaxing in the evening and hosting dinners by candlelight. The couple also delight in the sight of their young son playing on the terrace as he discovers the wonders of nature all around him. "Even though we have a glassed-in back

porch," Keith says, "there's something different about being outdoors, under the sky and stars."

The best garden rooms make friends and family feel right at home. To create an intimate atmosphere, the Keegans enclosed their terrace with living walls of plants and flower-filled window boxes. Furnishing the space are all the trappings of a cozy interior—vintage accessories, comfortable seating, and overstuffed throw pillows. An old chaise longue serves as a daybed in one corner; a nearby fountain gurgling in an urn provides soothing background noise.

Anchoring the room is a brick floor in a herringbone pattern, a beautiful treatment that is easy to install and maintain. Keith tackled the project himself, laying the bricks on a foundation of crushed limestone and mason's sand. Though it was chosen because it complements the exterior of the house, brick is also a durable material that will see the family through many years of use. "If you do it right," Keith says, "a brick terrace lasts indefinitely."

A weathered table, opposite, raises a display of architectural features and metal urns to eye level; when guests are due for dinner, it is cleared to double as a sideboard. A mirror, above, serves as a privacy screen and also makes the terrace appear much larger than it actually is.

A sandstone border surrounds the 24-by-18-foot terrace, providing a ledge for plants in pots and box planters. The space is furnished with a variety of auction and flea-market finds, including a steamer chair that originally sat on the deck of the Queen Elizabeth. Some other comfortable seating options are a park bench and an outdoor daybed softened with a duvet and vintage textiles. When friends visit, the adults lounge on the terrace and the children romp out on the lawn. The portico in the background serves as an open-air gardening shed.

THE GARDEN SEAT

The author Rudyard Kipling once mused that no garden was ever made by sitting in the shade. This may be true, but many a garden has been admired from a well-placed garden seat. From Claude Monet's beloved Giverny to Central Park in New York City, benches have long been a favorite perch for relaxation, observation, and contemplation. While they're often positioned to capture a picturesque view, they can fulfill a variety of other roles as well.

A formal Chippendale-style bench at the end of a path doubles as a resting place and as a piece of sculpture. A primitive country piece on a porch provides a sturdy surface for potting plants or for propping up your feet after tending the vegetable garden. Placing an old-fashioned park bench near a children's play area allows parents to share some private time while keeping an eye on the kids. If you're counting on a bench to provide a place to linger, select a comfortable design—stone or cast-iron benches make beautiful accents, but they weren't designed with relaxation in mind.

Whether you choose a colorful new bench or one that has long lived outdoors, a garden seat supplies entrancing visual pleasure. Painted furniture in blue or green always works in a natural setting, but don't be shy with other colors. A Creamsicle-colored bench, opposite, invites guests to stroll up and take a seat in a cozy cottage garden. Walk around your property to find creative spots for benches: A bench swing, above, allows clear views of a meadow. An English-style bench, following pages, crowns a hillside garden.

THE GARDEN TABLE

There's something about dining outdoors that makes the food taste just a little bit fresher and the company seem even more convivial. Every garden should have a dining area, whether it's a secluded nook for breakfast or a roomy spot for entertaining a big crowd. Dining on a terrace is practical because the kitchen is usually within easy reach, but transporting a table and chairs well out into the garden makes the most ordinary meal feel extraordinary. And there's no need to limit yourself to a picnic—dress the table with elegant stemware, colorful pottery, freshly cut flowers, candles, and crisp linens. Make the whole garden an enchanted dining room.

Keep comfort and ease in mind. For daytime meals in warm weather, choose a shaded site—pay attention to how the sun will shift—and try to take advantage of areas that are open to a breeze. Lightweight folding chairs are ideal for outdoor entertaining. They can be whisked inside if rain clouds appear or rearranged to form impromptu seating areas.

Lightweight café chairs, above, can easily be wiped dry if there's a shower before a springtime luncheon; they also fold up for tidy storage in winter. A garden urn, opposite, makes an elegant tableside wine cooler for an alfresco dinner. For a large party, ice down bottled drinks in a wheelbarrow, galvanized metal tubs, or a big stoneware crock.

During the heat of the summer, the most pleasurable outdoor meals often take place after the sun goes down. If you enjoy entertaining under the stars, effective lighting is essential. Remember that the prettiest ambience is created if you avoid glaring lights. Elegant lanterns of wrought iron, opposite, or frosted blown glass, right, bring the gentle illumination of candle-light and a touch of refinement to the outdoors. Use common sense when hanging them from pergolas, porches, or tree limbs.

a garden room

combines the comforts of home with **the infinite beauty** of the **natural world**

A California patio features a glass-topped stone capital for a dining table and a medley of vintage lanterns for illumination at twilight. The birdhouses attract winged wildlife yet also serve as folk-art accessories. The canopy of tree limbs suggests a ceiling, while the variety of plants carries texture and color throughout the room.

a place to
wander

A garden without paths must of necessity be admired from a distance. Add passageways, however, and it becomes a gateway to the many marvels of nature. Regardless of the hour, a stroll through the garden presents a host of discoveries. And, just as

the interior of a home needs hallways, a garden needs pathways that link outdoor living spaces.

Think of paths as avenues and side streets. Main thoroughfares—generally those that begin at the front and back doors of a house—are traditionally the widest. Paths that branch off to a shed or to a secluded seat can be narrower and more rustic.

Repositioning a path can be costly and time-consuming, so give placement plenty of forethought. Sketch out a plan on paper; then, before breaking ground, walk the route often. The material you choose will set the mood: A walkway of geometric paving stones has a formal feel, as does a corridor of mani-

cured lawn bordered by flower beds. Stepping-stones are more relaxed. A flooring of pine needles, moss, or wood chips evokes a woodland setting. When designing a main thoroughfare, keep the architectural style of your house in mind. A brick walkway complements the elegance of a colonial home, while a rugged fieldstone path may be more fitting for a farmhouse.

Edging a paved walkway up to the front door with potted plants, opposite, creates an inviting, embracing approach. Parallel clipped hedges, above, also signal an unmistakable entry; the stone birdbath provides focus and sharpens the perspective of the view.

THE EFFECT OF
A WOODEN FENCE

Regardless of the style, a wooden fence brings intimacy and structure to a garden. Choose the type that best suits your needs:

A PICKET FENCE has been a sentimental favorite since colonial times. It can be rustic if fashioned from weathered wood or formal if painted stark white and accented with finials.

LATTICE FENCING is the ideal backdrop for flowering vines. It also admits breezes and, when the sun is low, dappled light.

THE POST-AND-RAIL FENCE has long been a countryside staple. The open design makes any garden feel larger, and the weathered wood is as charming a companion to colorful flowers as it is to autumn leaves.

TALL PRIVACY FENCES provide security or block unsightly views. Their appearance can be softened by covering sections of a board fence with latticework and vines.

lead the way
on stairs
and paths
with groups of
shapely
clay pots
or rustic
watering
cans

Contrast is the secret to creating artful displays. An assortment of plants in deep verdant tones, opposite, offsets the coolness of curved gray steps. Watering cans sprouting petunias and phlox, right, bring life and cheerful color to a sturdy, plain staircase.

relaxing
the structure of an
elegant
sanctuary

every garden conveys a mood as soon as you begin to explore it. Some are so casual, you want to pull on a pair of faded jeans and stretch out on the grass. Others are so formal that they seem to require that you dress in your Sunday best for a tour of the parterres. The garden of Robert Jakob and David White exists happily between those two extremes. The look of the property is elegant, but the mood is welcoming and relaxed.

Located in East Hampton, New York, overlooking Accabonac Harbor, the garden occupies what was once a brambly wooded site. Now tended and mature, the grounds are punctuated by discreet elements that add beauty as well as a sense of structure and movement. For

example, large terra-cotta pots holding lemon, bay, and olive trees are arranged to frame paths and door-ways. "I wanted to create something that I might have seen in Italy," Jakob says, describing the inspiration behind the design. "I have a longing to be in Italy."

An Italianate garden would seem incomplete without classical ornament. Years ago, Jakob bought four antique columns at auction. Now in his garden, two columns support an arbor, one holds soap within reach of an outdoor shower, and another points sky-ward from the flower garden. The bases and capitals are handsome pedestals for pots of herbs and annuals.

An artist, Jakob has a passion for design that

naturally extends to the garden. Many gardens dazzle the eye with vibrant color or flamboyant decoration, but his is a study in restraint. An allée leads down to the harbor, but it is formed from casual mounds of bay-berry rather than strict rows of tall trees. "I go one way in formalizing things," Jakob explains, "and then I take two steps back."

A highlight of the garden is a set of four antique limestone columns, bases, and capitals that Jakob discovered at auction. One of the columns, opposite, adds verticality to the flower garden. Outside his studio, above, a capital supports a piece of driftwood to form a step.

An informal allée of bayberry
and cedar pays homage to
Italianate design. Jakob chose
bayberry and cedar because they
mimic the look of laurel and
cypress. The tree at the end of
the allée is a native beech that
the owners found when they
cleared the overgrown grounds
twenty years ago; they have
watched it grow from a small
tree into a beautiful focal point.
A favorite spot for casual meals
in summer, the lawn features
lightweight furniture that can
be moved around to make the
most of sun and shade.

THE GARDEN GATE

The entrance to a garden is as important as the front door of a house. It is almost always the first thing that visitors see, and it foretells what they will find on the other side of the threshold. A rose-covered archway may suggest that a cottage garden lies ahead, while an ornate wrought-iron gate hints at formal plantings.

On the perimeter of a property, a garden gate provides security when closed and an invitation to enter when left ajar. But gates can do more than that, and they do not have to be limited to the perimeter of your property. Positioned in the midst of a garden, they can add a feeling of privacy to a secluded spot or lend significance to a simple garden pathway. And, thanks to human nature, they also arouse curiosity, for everyone loves to sneak a peek through an open gate.

Installed within the garden, gates and fences define style as well as spaces. An impressive iron gate made of countless curlicues, left, adds dimension to lush plantings and a curving stone path. Who could resist exploring what lies around the bend?

THE BEAUTY OF ORNAMENTAL IRONWORK

From the villas of Renaissance Italy to the French Quarter of New Orleans, ironwork has embellished many gardens over the centuries. Whether old or new, fanciful wrought iron is one of the strongest elements you can add to a garden. The elegant filigree enriches the surroundings, yet the dark tone of the metal ensures that there is no visual competition. Instead, it seems to disappear as soon as it's noticed. The open design provides little privacy, but its presence imparts dignity to any space. If an ironwork fence seems too grand, consider adding a pair of brick columns to a hedge and hanging a wrought-iron gate between them.

Every garden entrance, no matter how humble or grand, sends a message to the outside world. A rustic twig gate, opposite, invites passersby to slow down and savor an herb garden, while a tall wooden door, right, signals that privacy is desired. Unpainted wood weathers over time and will visually fade away in natural surroundings. A colorfully painted gate, on the other hand, provides a vivid gesture that brightens the landscape. To establish a distinct connection between house and garden, paint your gate to match your front door, shutters, or trim.

a door
to the garden
can hint at what lies beyond
or keep it a wonderful secret

Pathways may lead the way to spectacular settings or to quiet nooks meant purely for solitude. When planning destinations in your garden, be sure to carve out spaces for enjoying favorite pastimes. This Colorado garden combines the owner's love of plants with a passion for model trains. A miniature locomotive winds through borders of pink asters, sweet alyssum, dwarf zinnias, and blooming oregano.

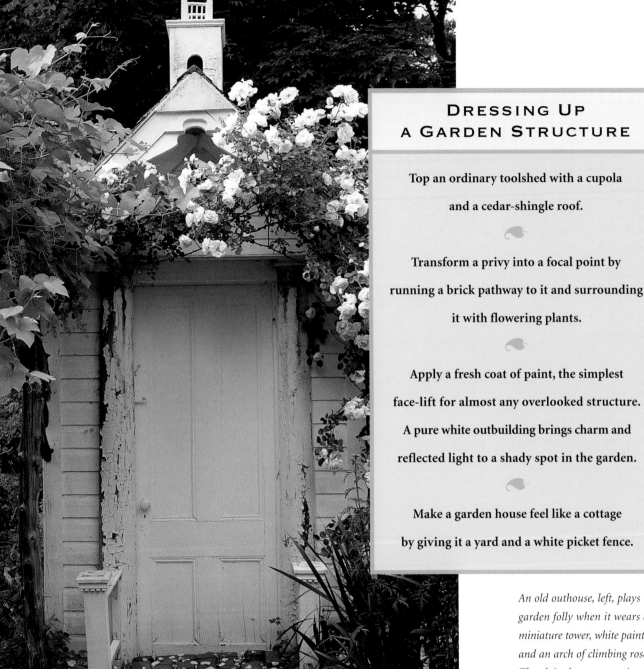

DRESSING UP A GARDEN STRUCTURE

Top an ordinary toolshed with a cupola
and a cedar-shingle roof.

❧

Transform a privy into a focal point by
running a brick pathway to it and surrounding
it with flowering plants.

❧

Apply a fresh coat of paint, the simplest
face-lift for almost any overlooked structure.
A pure white outbuilding brings charm and
reflected light to a shady spot in the garden.

❧

Make a garden house feel like a cottage
by giving it a yard and a white picket fence.

*An old outhouse, left, plays
garden folly when it wears a
miniature tower, white paint,
and an arch of climbing roses.
The plain door to a potting
shed, opposite, beckons with
a vintage sprinkler "wreath."*

detail and
ornament

Build the prettiest house on the block, and it's still just a house. Fill it with your own possessions, and it becomes a home. The same principle applies in the great outdoors. You can carve out a beautiful spot in the garden, but it doesn't become a garden room until you

furnish it with comfortable seating, atmosphere-enhancing accessories, and cherished collections.

Approach the accessorizing of an outdoor room as you would any interior decorating project. Begin by choosing a mood: Will it be formal or casual, traditional or a little offbeat? Do you prefer the romantic look of wicker or the clean lines of modern? Then choose a color scheme. Remember, the garden is a wonderful place to express your individuality, so experiment with hues that you might not go for inside the house, whether neutral or wildly bold.

As you proceed, let imagination be your guide. Garden ornament can be anything that piques your interest—a sundial or a bee skep, an old nursery sign, an Adirondack chair that reveals many layers of paint, a collection of colorful sap buckets transformed into planters. In just the right spot, a wheelbarrow or a rake is as decorative as it is functional. And don't forget the most natural accessory of all—foliage chosen to bring a variety of colors, shapes, and textures to the landscape.

An imaginative container gardener can transform empty pots into showpieces by varying the colors, textures, and heights of the plants. A chartreuse sweet potato vine, opposite, stands out in a grouping of ornamental grasses and variegated foliage. All but the largest potted plants can be shifted around a terrace to create different effects or placed on top of a table, above, to brighten a weekend brunch.

a ledge
lined with
**flower-filled
pots**
provides a
**glorious
view**
from both
sides of the
window

*Edging a window with plants
elevates the garden and enlivens
the exterior of the house. In
lieu of window boxes planted
like beds, bracket shelves, left,
support rows of terra-cotta pots.
By using individual containers,
you can easily substitute a plant
if one begins to fade or rearrange
the entire display to suit your
whim. Including some slightly
oversize pots, opposite, results in
displays with added abundance.*

THE PORTABLE FLOWERPOT

Containers are the ultimate garden accessory because they marry form and function. An aged terra-cotta pot or a mossy stone urn is a beautiful object even without a topiary or a mix of annuals. Traditional receptacles such as glazed flowerpots make colorful accent pieces, but nearly anything can be a planter. Vintage household objects, such as a washtub or a stoneware crock, lend country charm, as does a half-barrel, a milk pail, or a fruit crate.

Experiment with placement: A pair of urns brings prominence to a garden entry, while a cluster of pots on a deck creates the illusion of a teeming perennial bed. Flower-filled containers also make charming markers along a temporary pathway carved out for a garden party. Often, the best decorative effect stems from pure simplicity—a stack of empty pots inside a garden shed or a solitary urn proudly standing at the end of a vista.

CREATIVE CONTAINER GARDENING

When seeking out unique containers, keep these tips in mind:

GOOD DRAINAGE is essential, so look for pieces with holes in the bottom or to which holes can be added. You can easily drill or punch drainage holes through wood or metal; glass items like milk bottles make better vases.

WOOD PLANTERS should be lined with heavy plastic to protect them from moisture. A rusty metal container also needs to be lined because rust alters the pH balance of soil.

LARGE POTS are dramatic in the garden, but they eat up vast amounts of potting soil. Use less soil by filling the bottom of an oversize container with broken clay pots or packing peanuts.

Just because you're decorating in the garden doesn't mean that your accessories have to be garden-variety. An old graniteware coffeepot, above, makes a charming flowerpot, while terra-cotta boots, opposite, become unexpected sculpture in a bed of ferns.

DESIGN IDEAS FOR THE KITCHEN GARDEN

Accessorize your herb or vegetable garden with produce in mind: handpainted herb markers, old farmstand signs, or images of fruit that anticipate the crop.

Add visual interest—and the convenience of harvesting at arm's length—by creating a series of small square or rectangular beds. Frame them with decorative edging or pave the adjacent walkways with salvaged brick.

Build tepee-shaped trellises out of willow branches or bamboo for sweet peas, green beans, and other climbers.

Fill empty spaces with a collection of glass cloches or terra-cotta rhubarb forcers for an old-fashioned look; they are too attractive to be stored away when not on active duty.

Recycled elements bring just the
right sense of thrifty practicality
to a kitchen garden. Even an old
wagon wheel can enjoy a new
life in an herb garden separating
different varieties of thyme, left,
or other low-growing herbs. A
salvaged window makes a great
cover for a cold frame, above,
which is used to protect young
plants during the chilly days of
late winter and early spring.

Garden sculpture doesn't need to be high art. Who could present more country charm to passersby than a scarecrow, left, taking a break with his own shovel at his side? When they're not performing their natural duties, old painted wheelbarrows, right, become bold, colorful sculptures against the gray-wood fence that screens a composting area. A chorus line of metal lawn chairs from the 1950s, following pages, adds vibrant color to an autumn celebration held beneath the limbs of a 200-year-old ash. When the party gets under way, the seating can be reassembled to form conversation areas.

sometimes
the most beautiful view
appears when we
turn and see a trusted,
well-worn tool

ONE-OF-A-KIND FINDS

Ornament can evoke a variety of feelings. A humorous folk-art figure may elicit a chuckle, while a bench from Grandmother's garden revives treasured memories. An aged staddle stone recalls the English countryside; a stone lantern suggests a tranquil Japanese garden.

A well-placed artifact can attract attention away from an undesirable view or make a pretty section of the garden even more charming.

unique accessories make a garden memorable and truly your own

Partially hidden ornaments sometimes create the most enchantment. Visitors will delight in rounding a bend to discover a carved marble maiden or in spotting a terra-cotta turtle at pond's edge.

If you've always wanted a theme garden, strive for subtlety. Classical statuary is magical in the proper setting, but a lack of restraint will make your grounds feel like an outdoor museum or a Las Vegas casino. Let your garden reflect your own personality, and avoid one-stop shopping. Taking the time to scour antiques shows, estate sales, and out-of-the-way shops is the secret to unearthing distinctive pieces.

Ornament has long been used to create fantasy in the garden. If you want to attract fairies or keep evil spirits at bay, a gazing globe, opposite, just might do the trick. Popular in the Victorian era and beyond, this fabled garden accent is best showcased high on a pedestal to reflect the beauty of the surroundings.

Putting a face—literally—on a garden is a marvelous way to personalize it. Search for clever places to install some friendly countenances. A fanciful folk-art duo fashioned of scraps of wire and wood, opposite, asks for nothing but a smile in return as it keeps watch from the corner of a shingled outbuilding. A cherub face, right, becomes a guardian angel when it is hung from the perfect spot on a weathered wall; tendrils of Lysimachia n. 'Aurea' hang on either side like tresses.

wit and whimsy
in a folk-art
garden

Some people comb country auctions for old garden implements, while others travel to far-flung countries to seek out exotic finds. To Jeanelle Myers, however, garden ornament can simply be junk rescued from the town dump. "I've always liked the idea of using other people's trash," she says. "I don't like to throw things away."

Both an artist and a professional gardener, Jeanelle has a knack for transforming trash and other found objects into garden treasures. Her quirky folk-art garden is full of surprises: American flags hang from old fishing poles, recycled copper pipes form a garden gate, and pieces of crystal dangle from upturned tree roots. Lounging along a fence is a

clique of female wooden figures with bottle caps for eyes, bedsprings for hair, and clothing fashioned from fishing net.

When Jeanelle set out to create flower beds, she wanted to edge them with a recycled material that would be useful and pretty. Her solution was porcelain and stoneware plates in a variety of patterns and colors. "I discovered that you can get plates at yard sales for very little money," she says, "but you can get them at the dump for free." Held in place with PVC edging, the secondhand dishes help keep soil contained while bringing a lighthearted touch to the formal geometric beds at the same time. Teacups, saucers, and pitchers are found elsewhere in the garden, perhaps holding up a flowerpot or serving as a miniature piece of sculpture.

Jeanelle approaches her garden as a work of art and enjoys leaving her signature on the world around her. She's been tending the grounds for a decade but never tires of creating vignettes. "Every fall I tear a bunch of it apart and move stuff around," she says. "I like to make things, and I like to make things change."

In this Long Island, New York, garden, recycled materials enjoy a second life as unique garden ornament. Watering is never a chore with this handsome metalwork gate, opposite, that doubles as a gardenside spigot. Copper pipes and an antique faucet distinguish the piece. A cheerful lad named Junior, below, brightens an asparagus patch with his vibrant color and amusing features. His knickers are painted cedar shingles; his hair is twisted telephone wire.

After scraping off its reflective backing, Jeanelle placed the lens of an old klieg light, above, on a chafing-dish base and filled it with water to make an ingenious sculpture. A folksy birdbath, opposite, is actually a large terra-cotta pot saucer that has been set inside the grill of an old charcoal stove.

GARDEN STATUARY

In centuries past, statuary was an indulgence for the elite. Elegant figures embellished royal pleasure grounds like Versailles, but the hand-carved works were beyond the reach of average people. In the nineteenth century, however, the widespread production of artificial stone made statuary affordable for many.

Created from a clay- or cement-based formula, artificial stone was molded into every conceivable form, from gods and goddesses to ducks and comical wood sprites. Particularly popular a century ago were cast-cement ornaments shaped like fruit- and flower-filled baskets. Antique examples tend to come at a high price today, but reproductions are readily available. Allow them to weather for a few years and they will appear as longtime denizens of your garden. To cultivate the growth of moss, try mixing yogurt or manure with water and applying it to a piece. If you rub it with moss, keep it moist, and set it in the shade, nature should take its course in record time.

CREATURES REAL AND FAUX

Habitats for wildlife lend picturesque charm to the garden, whether or not they are actually occupied. Set a bee skep on a bench or top a cedar post with a weathered birdhouse.

Small animals cast from metal or carved of wood are especially enchanting to children. Set a green-painted frog by a water garden or let a squirrel keep watch atop a fence post.

Attract real creatures by providing trees and shrubs for shelter, a year-round water source, and flowers, berries, nuts, and other foods.

Because they look like carved stone, cement ornaments are a natural fit in the garden. Formal shapes, such as flower-filled urns and classical statues, establish a sophisticated mood. This alert rabbit, however, offers a more playful surprise in a flower bed bordering a grove of birches.

Bee skeps and birdhouses have become icons of the country garden. Coiled straw skeps were a favorite honeybee hideaway prior to the nineteenth century, but today they serve primarily as decorative accessories. Here, an old-fashioned still life is created by lining up a white-washed skep with other garden accents on an old worn bench. Birdhouses range from rustic to refined, but safety features are more important than aesthetics if you hope to shelter winged wildlife. Gaps between the roof and the walls will abet air circulation; holes drilled in the floor allow rainwater to drain.

99

SYLVAN SCULPTURE

Though the nobility of Renaissance Italy would certainly disagree, garden sculpture doesn't have to be cast in stone. It can just as easily be a piece of driftwood discovered on a beach, a retired weather vane, a willow plant support, or a birdbath fashioned from recycled materials.

When selecting a substantial piece, imagine how it will look in five years or even further down the road. If left untreated, wood weathers to a wonderful silvery gray, while bronze and lead take on a dramatic streaked patina that only time can render.

Garden ornament should always enhance rather than compete with the beauty of a space. A piece of sculpture is in the wrong spot if it jolts the eye or attracts attention away from your prizewinning roses. An ornate marble statue usually looks best against a simple backdrop of greenery, whereas an obelisk or earthenware jar makes the biggest impact if it stands in architectural contrast to a tangle of colorful perennials.

A dramatic piece of driftwood rises from a sea of santolina, right, in a serenely composed garden. The jagged limbs of the found art are an effective foil for the strict geometry of the trellis, and the gray tones of all the woods contribute to the setting's tranquillity.

When nothing in the garden points skyward, we tend to focus on the ground and miss some of the best views. Vertical ornament can be a humble element borrowed from nature, such as a pair of twisted California bay saplings, left, surrounded by stalks of clary. Or it can be majestic, like an armillary sphere, right, set on a classical column.

a well-placed
piece of
sculpture
brings a
sense of
permanence to the garden

Garden accessories will assume different duties and moods as the seasons change. During the summer, this urn might serve as home for a cascading plant with colorful flowers, but in winter it becomes a regal focal point on top of the stone wall. Whether it's a fancy urn or a primitive birdhouse, an object takes on added importance when show-cased on some sort of pedestal.

THE GARDEN IN WINTER

Chilly temperatures and shorter days signal that it's almost time to shelve the gardening gear and head indoors. But the garden should not be forgotten. A sleeping garden can be just as beautiful as one in full bloom if it's furnished with winter in mind. During most of the year, ornament plays second fiddle to flowers and foliage. But as leaves drop and perennials are cut back, those decorative elements have to play more dramatic roles. Select pieces with interesting lines that will enliven the landscape, and make sure they are hardy enough to stand up to colder weather.

Plants with colorful bark or berries brighten dreary days, and a dark-lead statue will provide stunning contrast to icy surroundings. When dusted with snow, a birdhouse becomes as charming as a country cottage. And what should you do with those two weather-beaten chairs out on the lawn? Pull on your woolens, take a seat in the sun, and dream up new plans while you wait for the garden to awake in the spring.

Left out to overwinter along a hedge, a handsome pair of Adirondack chairs provide a bold architectural element and a reminder that warm weather will return. Their appearance is always welcoming, even to falling leaves and dustings of snow.

the elegant form of an urn
or the graceful back of a garden bench
avails itself each year
of winter's icy magic

resources

SUPPLIERS AND CATALOGS

AMBIENTE
Northfield, IL
(847) 441-5902

Iron garden furniture; to the trade only

THE AMERICAN FOLK ART FURNITURE CO.
RR 3, Box 1647
Monkey Island, OK 74331
(918) 257-4062/(888) 649-7973
www.afastudio.com

Hand-carved, custom-designed garden furniture and decorative items; catalog

BAUER'S MARKET & NURSERY
221 South 2nd Street
La Crescent, MN 44947
(507) 895-4583
www.bauersmarket.com

Seasonal decorative items for the garden

THE CLINGING VINE
Onalaska, WI
(608) 526-2605

Garden trellises

EAST HAMPTON GARDENS
4 Gingerbread Lane
East Hampton, NY 11937
(631) 324-1133
www.ehgardens.com

Decorative items and antiques for the garden

GARDENER'S SUPPLY CO.
128 Intervale Road
Burlington, VT 05401
(800) 944-2250
www.gardeners.com

Bird feeders, statues, sundials, and other garden ornaments; catalog

GOOD DIRECTIONS, INC.
20 Commerce Drive
Danbury, CT 06810
(800) 852-3002/(203) 743-3775
www.gooddirections.com

Weather vanes, garden stakes, and other decorative items for the garden; catalog

POTLUCK STUDIOS
23 Main Street
Accord, NY 12404
(914) 626-2300
www.potluck@frontiernet.net

Assorted glazed pots; to the trade only; call for catalog and local availability

RUE DE FRANCE
(800) 777-0998
www.ruedefrance.com

Outdoor furniture and garden ornaments imported from France; catalog

SUNBRELLA/ GLEN RAVEN CUSTOM FABRICS LLC
www.sunbrella.com

Textiles for outdoor use; visit Web site for local availability

THE TIN BIN
20 Valley Road
Neffsville, PA 17601
(717) 569-6210
www.thetinbin.com

18th-century lighting reproductions in brass, copper, and tin

Garden Antiques Dealers

Balsamo Antiquités
Route 199
Pine Plains, NY 12567
(518) 398-9066

Canyan Antiques Ltd.
192 East 70th Street
New York, NY 10021
(212) 988-8340

Cottage & Camp Antiques
99 Tinker Street
Woodstock, NY 12498
(914) 679-6499

Country Loft Antiques
557 Main Street South
Woodbury, CT 06798
(203) 266-4500

Scott Estepp
P.O. Box 19669
Cincinnati, OH 45219
(513) 221-2713

Joan Evans Antiques
Antiques & Artisans Center
69 Jefferson Street
Stamford, CT 06902
(203) 327-6022

The Finnegan Gallery
2030 North Mohawk
Chicago, IL 60614
(312) 951-6858

By appointment

Gray Gardens
461 Broome Street
New York, NY 10013
(212) 966-7116

Marston Luce Antiques
1314 21st Street NW
Washington, DC 20036
(202) 775-9460
www.marstonluce.com

Pam & Gene Martine
P.O. Box 787
Greenwich, CT 06836
(203) 869-7900

Judith & James Milne
506 East 74th Street
New York, NY 10021
(212) 472-0107

Salvage One
1524 Sangamon Street
Chicago, IL 60608
(312) 733-0098

Linda & Howard Stein
P.O. Box 58
Solebury, PA 18963
(215) 297-0606

Frank Swim Antiques
430 Warren Street
Hudson, NY 12534
(518) 822-0411

Ronnie & Guy Weil
P.O. Box 583
New Hope, PA 18938
(215) 862-9421

Dan Wilson, Inc.
200 South West Street
Raleigh, NC 27603
(919) 833-4700

Yardart
2188 ½ Sutter Street
San Francisco, CA 94115
(415) 346-6002